Marketing to the Invisible Investor

Lessons in Digital Marketing for Financial Companies

Paul Das

Published by New Generation Publishing in 2021

Copyright © Paul Das 2021

First Edition

The author asserts the moral right under the Copyright, Designs and Patents Act 1988 to be identified as the author of this work.

All Rights reserved. No part of this publication may be reproduced, stored in a retrieval system or transmitted, in any form or by any means without the prior consent of the author, nor be otherwise circulated in any form of binding or cover other than that which it is published and without a similar condition being imposed on the subsequent purchaser.

ISBN   978-1-80031-059-9

www.newgeneration-publishing.com

Foreword

Paul is the rare breed of [marketing leader] - someone who understands the big picture, can translate that into realistic marketing activities and knows that it's all about bringing (sales & marketing) people together to achieve great things.

This book is written in the style you'd expect from Paul and it cuts through the usual theory of marketing written by folk who haven't actually had to make any of it work. He takes every digital marketing topic that matters and walks you through why and how you should do it.

Apart from that, it's simply a good read for anyone in the asset management industry (or beyond) who wants a guide to doing better marketing and sales (in that order). It's a recommended read from me.

Andrew Scott
MD
White Marble

With Thanks to Charles Barnick

Introduction - It Starts With Tea And Biscuits...

I've seen it time and again.

And it's tragic.

When hard times hit, in the name of cost-cutting, an unforgivable decision is made.

Tea and biscuits in meetings are banned. It's water all round.

But next up, the marketing department usually takes a hit. The thinking goes that this is an expendable part of the business, which you can afford to do away with at the drop of a hat and still turn a profit.

That's why marketing teams take such a beating when a cost-cutting fervour starts. Even in times of plenty, marketing is often seen as something of a frippery – an expensive thing you have because everyone else has got one, but you don't really need. Like the business equivalent of a bread maker.

And in harsh economic times, the marketing head quickly appears on the corporate axeman's block to ease the pressure on other departments deemed more relevant and important.

But this is a stupid thing to do.

Marketing is essential for any business in any sector – during both growth and recession. In fact, studies show that the firms that bounce back best from recessions are those that maintain and even increase their marketing budgets.

The lesson from your cereal bowl

To give you an example, during the Great Depression of the 1920s American cereal manufacturer Post – the biggest in the sector at the time – responded to falling sales by slashing its marketing budget. By contrast, a smaller company – Kellogg's – did the opposite and doubled its marketing spend in a bid to attract new customers. It invested heavily in ads and introduced a new brand called Rice Krispies, complete with 'Snap, crackle and pop' slogan. This allowed Kellogg's to steal a march on its rival and helped it to become the leading company in the breakfast cereal market.

Now, I know you don't sell cereal. This book concerns the fund and asset management sector, and specifically how you can use digital marketing techniques to raise and retain assets.

But I'm going to start by talking about the wider importance of marketing to an organisation. At the time of writing, the global economy is reeling from the Covid-19 pandemic and harsh times are coming, so it's more important than ever to make this point.

The wise old man of Coke

Sergio Zyman, former Chief Marketing Officer of The Coca-Cola Company, once said this:

"The sole purpose of marketing is to sell more to more people, more often and at higher prices."

The key word there is 'sell'. But too many people forget that marketing is ultimately about sales, which is why so many senior executives misunderstand its role and importance.

It's obvious that without sales you haven't got a business. But without an effective marketing department you haven't got a sales department.

You may get by, for a time, but without a capable marketing team driving long-term growth, you are doomed to fail.

It's the job of the sales team to make and seal deals, but that is far from the whole story. The marketing department is there to sow the seeds of these deals and attract prospects in the first place, so they are primed and ready to act when they reach the last stage of the buying process, which is talking to sales.

And this is especially true in finance, where buying decisions are often long, drawn out processes. Nobody makes a major investment decision about which fund or asset manager to use on a whim – they're not buying a packet of sweets. When it comes to the crunch, for a prospective investor to choose your firm your marketing department must first have done its job by promoting, educating, and instilling trust.

So, marketing is vital to the success of your business.

Actually let me rephrase that – *good* marketing is vital to the success of your business.

And today, more than ever, good marketing means digital marketing. People live an increasingly digital life – they buy, socialise, keep up with the news, and entertain themselves online.

And it's online where you'll find your prospective investors and connect with your existing clients.

But what exactly does good digital marketing look like?

This book is a comprehensive guide to the whys, whats and hows of this subject.

I'm going to look at digital marketing and how it applies to the fund and asset management sector. I'm also going to show you how to analyse the results of your digital marketing efforts – and how these two things combined can help you to raise and retain assets under management.

Effective digital marketing requires hard work and dedication and can be complicated, but the principles that underly it are relatively simple and don't require special knowledge or talent to understand. And knowing what you need to do – rather than blundering around in the dark – makes life so much easier (and more profitable).

I hope you enjoy this book. Nothing that follows is academic or overly technical – anyone can understand and act upon my advice. To get the best from it, I suggest you give each point some thought. How does it relate to me and my firm? Is this something I can apply? Am I doing something obviously wrong?

Above all, I hope that what I tell you helps you with your digital marketing efforts and adds value to your business.

Chapter 1 - The World Has Changed

The rise of the invisible investor and what it means for your business

As I write, in early 2021, Covid-19 continues to spread across the world.

But whether you read my words in 2021 or later, you will be dealing with the effects of this awful virus in some way or another.

Because, with all the lockdowns and lockouts that have been the response to the pandemic, there has been an inevitable switch to doing things digitally. Email traffic and data usage has soared, and Zoom is no longer just a perky verb or a fondly remembered ice lolly – it's the world's favourite communication choice.

And in the financial sector, just like everywhere else, people are communicating online, rather than meeting in person. No more chats in the office, long lunches, or deals sealed in the hospitality suite at Twickenham.

It's all been digital.

But I bet my bottom bitcoin that many in the fund and asset management sector will ignore this digital shift and, when they can, carry on as before.

They'll think that face-to-face schmoozing, advising, and lunching will return and they can kick digital marketing back into the hedge where it belongs.

Big mistake.

Because the world didn't just change due to Covid.

In fact, the digital transition amongst investors has been ongoing for a couple of decades – the global pandemic merely accelerated it.

You only have to look at wider society to grasp this point. And, to illustrate it, please come along with me to the humble British pub.

The virtual pint

In the UK, until about thirty years ago, pubs were everywhere. Even the smallest village had at least one pub and they were packed every night of the week. These hostelries were mostly old-fashioned spit and sawdust 'boozers' where you went for a drink and a chat. If you wanted something to eat, the best you'd get was a packet of stale crisps and a pickled egg.

Fast forward to 2020 and the pub sector has been decimated. Pubs have closed in their thousands and in villages, towns and city centres across the country, boarded up inns are a depressingly familiar sight. And many of those that remain are gastropubs, with nothing to distinguish them from a restaurant apart from the old pub sign swinging outside the door.

Now there are many reasons for this – the UK banned smoking inside back in 2007, which meant your local stopped looking like a scene from The Towering Inferno, but also wiped out the time-honoured tradition of a pint and a cigarette, causing many to stay at home. Equally, rising wholesale costs for alcohol, and increased rents forced many pubs out of business.

But one major culprit was and is social media. Why walk down to the pub in the wind and rain to meet friends, when you can crack open a can at home and chat to them on Facebook or in a WhatsApp group from the warmth and comfort of your living room?

Of course, it's not just pubs – it's everywhere. Why go into a bank to pay a bill when you can do it with a few clicks? Why go into a clothes store to buy that top, when you can just do it on their website? Why go to the music shop to buy an album when you can stream it on Spotify?

And there's the rub.

People can do a lot of what they used to do in person, digitally. They don't *have* to actually go anywhere or see anyone.

And finance is no different.

The invisible investor

Over the two decades since founding ProFundCom, I've seen our sector become increasingly – if gradually - reliant on digital marketing.

And Covid-19 has turbocharged that process. During lockdown, what was once a choice – doing things through a screen rather than in person – became a necessity. Even those who were used to face-to-face meetings with relationship managers were forced to do it online.

So, while the pandemic may not be the final nail in the coffin for the old way of doing things, the hammering has certainly started.

As I've just said, when the Covid crisis is over – and maybe when you're reading this it is – in-person events will run again, corporate hospitality will be up and going, and people will be traveling to meet their relationship manager face-to-face.

But for how long will all this continue in a way that's both profitable, sensible and sustainable?

The glaring truth is that, for many, the investor journey is now almost if not entirely digital. Unlike in the past, there is no linear process that progresses, basically, from first contact, to meeting with a relationship manager, to sale, to ongoing in-person meetings every quarter.

Even before Covid, this didn't appeal to the new breed of millennial and gen Z investors, who can't even remember a time before the internet. These people are used to the instant gratification offered by technology. When they want to buy something, Amazon delivers it the next day. When they want to eat, Deliveroo brings their favourite restaurant to the door. When they want to watch a film, Netflix et al have got whatever they want on demand.

So, there is a large chunk of your prospective and existing market who are more than likely to be 'invisible investors' – prospects and clients who you never even see. They follow an investor journey that's made up of multiple online interactions, starting from an introduction to your firm through some form of digital content.

And, thanks to Covid, the ranks of invisible investors will have been boosted considerably, as *everyone* can now see the ease and simplicity of digital interaction - and the genie is not going back into the bottle.

You must understand all this and realise that the days of knowing, seeing and engaging with investors in the traditional sense are largely gone.

But, how do you reach out to and connect with the invisible investor?

If you're doing the job of digital marketing properly, the invisible investor should encounter you everywhere – from your website, to emails, to social media, to blogs, and press pieces, all the way to the sale, which is maybe the only time that many investors will actually speak to someone in your firm.

Even post-sale this digital process should continue, through online onboarding, ongoing investment advice, regular account updates and even (if necessary) retention review.

And the new form of the investor journey has fundamentally changed the way that fund marketing must operate. In a digital age you need digital marketing content that engages with your prospects and existing clients where they want to find you – online.

On top of that, for digital fund marketing to succeed in its ultimate aim of raising and retaining assets, you must analyse the results of your efforts – and act on what you find.

So, you just need to get content in front of the people who may want to invest with you – and then look at how they are interacting with it.

Easy, right?

Not really. It may sound simple but that's why so many content marketing strategies are so ill-conceived and ineffective. For analysis – and digital marketing in general – to be effective, you need to be producing content that people want to digest and engage with, (which may sound like common sense but is a fact that's all too often ignored).

We'll come onto how to create quality content soon, but first let's think about those who you are trying to reach and are the source of investment – your prospects and clients.

Chapter 2 - The Search For Persona Grata

How to find and market to your target audience

We've established that digital is here to stay – and the web is where you will increasingly find and interact with your prospects and clients. Because the millennials and generation Xers who are coming through and forming your new client base live digital lives. They haven't got the time, inclination or need to do many things in person – and this includes receiving investment advice. So, they scour the web for information that guides a big financial decision - rather than relying on the advice of a relationship manager.

I know I referred to this new breed of digital investors as 'faceless' and 'invisible', but that's purely because you are unlikely to ever meet them in person. But it's vital to remember that they are still individuals – real people with names, jobs, families, and wants and needs that are unique to them.

Obvious, right?

Well, it is if you think about it. But way too many people in marketing are guilty of seeing their audience as a single, homogenous lump that needs no variation or subtlety when it comes to communications.

And this attitude gives rise to the 'spray and pray' approach to marketing, which works on the theory of sending out vast amounts of identical messages to everyone on a database, with the hope that some of it will stick.

And, of course, some of it will work – and lead to some sales. So, companies continue to use this approach, especially because sending out generic, untargeted content is quicker and easier than sending out quality, well-targeted pieces.

But any gain will be far outweighed by the fact that the vast majority of people will become fed up with the endless stream of unsolicited information, most of which has little to do with their interests and priorities. Spraying your marketing message out to anyone and everyone and hoping that the right someone will immediately come knocking at your door is not a long-term strategy.

The fact is, when you try to speak to everyone, most people stop listening. And, even worse, they lose any faith or trust they may have had in your firm – which is difficult, if not impossible, to win back.

Why you must target your communications

The alternative to the spray and pray approach is to send communications that are targeted to what the people you want to reach are actually interested in.

This has many advantages. The most obvious being that if you send people emails that are based upon what you know about them, then they are far more likely to read them. This is good news for your marketing efforts and your profit margins.

But there is also something deeper going on, as when you send more targeted messages then you also help to build a relationship with your prospect or client. For example, when someone reads an email that relates to what is important to them, then it says that you have taken the trouble to learn a bit about that person and that you are not going to insult their intelligence by simply chucking everything their way, with no thought to it being helpful or relevant.

By contrast, sending out content that *is* relevant to a person's interests suggests to them that you understand and value them. And this helps to build and maintain trust.

The importance of trust cannot be underestimated – and it's a theme I'll come back to later – as it is a vital step in *any* buying process. A company like the chocolate firm Cadbury, for instance, has built a business on trust. When someone walks into a shop and sees a new brand of Cadbury chocolate bar on the shelf, they buy it because they trust it's going to taste good. They have prior experience with Cadbury and they know it can be relied upon to deliver something delicious.

And the power of trust is magnified in any financial setting, as few people would give their money to a firm they don't trust.

The power of personas

The more closely you personalise your messages, and the more focused you are on who you want to attract and the more targeted your marketing is, the more successful you will be in winning clients and boosting AuM.

Given all that, it stands to reason that the more you know about your customers the more effectively you can communicate with them.

This obviously applies in any business, which is why companies across many sectors have long used statistical techniques to better understand client behaviour and then tailor their marketing efforts accordingly.

But fund marketing often lags behind in this regard, as both prospective and existing investors tend to be grouped according to their attitude to risk. Although this is important information, it's a very broad grouping and too general to deliver a truly personalised marketing service. For that, you need to dig deeper – and find out about a person's preferences across a range of factors, not just risk.

One way to do this is through client personas.

What exactly is a client persona?

In short, a client persona is a representation of the attitudes, goals and behaviour of a hypothesized group of customers – based on what you know about your existing clients.

This could cover their attitude to business, spending, saving, environmental causes and philanthropy – all things that could affect their financial choices and, crucially for you, where they choose to invest their money. It can also delve into age, gender, interests, family situation and more.

All this information is brought together to create a client persona. You can give them actual names, and even pictures, so you can visualise and empathise with the people you are targeting. Giving each persona a name also simplifies the project process for team members. For example, instead of referring to a group of prospects who are 'male clients aged 35 to 50 who live in the

London area and hold executive level positions in medium-sized corporations', you can simply talk about how best to market to 'David Sullivan'.

These fictional, generalised characters help you to understand your clients better and provide valuable insight into important factors such as needs, goals and behaviour patterns.

The theory behind all this is that by using what you know about your existing investors, you can map out how *potential* investors are likely to think and act. And that is incredibly useful for your marketing efforts, as you know the type of message that is likely to work with each person that comes onto your radar.

It's not fool proof, obviously, as everyone is an individual and there is no guarantee they will act in a certain way or react favourably to a certain type of message. But having client personas in place is far better than the alternative, which is either guessing at what to include in a message – or simply sending the same type or actual message to everyone in your database.

Using client personas makes it possible to draw up and execute more personalised marketing campaigns that are aimed at different groups, so you can create specific pieces of content for specific personas. For example, instead of sending the same lead nurturing emails to everyone in your database, you can segment by persona and tailor your messaging according to what you know appeals to each one.

Negative personas

You can take things a step further by creating negative personas, which are a representation of who you *don't* want as a client. This could be because of a low tolerance of risk, for example, or because you identify that persona as someone who sucks up a lot of time and effort without actually investing.

This enables you to weed out the 'bad apples' from the rest of your contacts, which can mean a lower cost-per-lead and cost-per-customer -- and boost efficiency and productivity, as you don't have to spend time chasing lost causes

How to create a persona

The easy way to establish a client persona?

Send out a questionnaire to all your existing investors. This will allow you to build an accurate picture of who they are and what they do as that will form the basis of your personas. For example, you would need to know:

- Personal background - age, family, marital status
- Educational background – qualifications, university attended (if any), field of study
- Size and sector of their employer

- Their role and position in the company
- Personal, professional and investment goals
- Attitude to risk

How many clients you engage with is up to you, but the more the better and the stronger your personas will be as a result.

But, although important, this method is a relatively blunt instrument (and is also extremely time consuming) as asking questions does not always give a reliable picture of more nuanced opinions, such as their attitude to money. Because, to be frank, people don't always tell the truth.

So, it's wise to combine it with other methods. In fact, there will be a wealth of useful information about your audience in the digital ether that is waiting to be collected and analysed. You can quickly discover things like buying preferences, where they live, where they were educated, which devices they like to use etc. This type of data can be gathered completely within the remit of GDPR and wider data regulations – and anonymised – so you are not breaking any rules.

Another useful method is to analyse the actual investment decisions your clients make, as this is proof of how they behave in certain situations, rather than how they – or you - think they'd behave.

Also, ask your sales team for feedback on how different types of clients and prospects interact. What generalisations can they make about certain groups of people on your database?

Once you have gone through this whole research stage, you'll have a strong body of raw material. You must bring all this information together to identify patterns and commonalities between certain types of people. This will allow you to draw up your client personas, and then you can slot in all your existing and prospective investors to the groups that they most closely match. You can then do the same for leads as they enter your database, which will guide what you send out to them.

Take your time

As with anything, the more you plan and prepare, the more value you will get from the process. Skimping on this in favour of rushing onto the messaging stage could cost you dear.

So, don't rush it when you actually create your personas – as this is the most vital part of it all. You must invest time and money into developing personas that are a strong and close match to various client groups. Then, before you start using your personas, ensure that everyone in your sales and marketing teams knows and understands each persona and the person that lies behind it.

There is no point in talking about how a particular email would appeal to 'Susan Griffin', for example, if nobody can picture who she is.

But when you have a range of personas in place that everybody knows about then you have a strong platform for developing content that these people want to read.

How do you know what they want?

But this presents a thorny problem, because how do you know for sure what someone at the other end of an email – or a social media page, website or any other channel for your communications - actually wants to read?

Client personas will give you an idea of who they are and what their preferences and interests are but, in all likelihood, nobody in your firm will ever have met this person.

One answer is digital analytics. Simply through the process of producing and sending out content you are giving yourself valuable data to analyse.

In its simplest terms, this means you must analyse the reaction to your content and use that to build up a picture of what that person is interested in – and what they simply ignore.

That will guide what you send them in the future, as you can concentrate on the topics and themes that you know they like and leave out those that they don't.

But I'm getting ahead of myself. To have enough engagement data to make analysis worthwhile, you must be creating and sending out content that is likely to be read in the first place. How do you do that? What do investors want to know about? What is the best way to present it?

The answers to these questions deserve a chapter of their own...

Chapter 3 - Content Is King (But Engagement Is Queen)

Understanding the content that people want to see

The phrase 'content is king' has been overused to the point of cliché. But do you know who first coined it?

Pat on the back if you said Bill Gates.

This was the title of a piece by Gates that appeared on the Microsoft website in 1996. In it, he predicted – amongst other things - that the supply of information or entertainment through content would be where the real money would be made on the internet.

And he's been proved right. YouTube, Facebook, and even Twitter, are largely content providers.

People go on there to watch and read content - and as a result advertisers pay handsomely to feature on these sites.

But it's not just the big boys who are in on the game. In his essay, Gates praised the democracy of the internet, saying that in the future no firm would be too small to partake in this content revolution. He saw that in time anyone with an internet connection would be able to create new and exciting things.

Again, spot on. His foresight was pretty remarkable given that, at the time, only about 1% of the world was online, connection speeds were at a snail's pace, and many people didn't even know what the internet was. Just a handful of companies actually had websites, so it would have been sensible to predict a future digital world in which big corporations would hold sway, much as the TV companies did.

But Gates realised that new and better technology would drive down costs and expand reach, so anyone could become author and influencer.

Today, companies big and small, across all sectors, pump websites and social media feeds full of content that's designed to attract and retain an audience, for the ultimate purpose of promoting their product or service.

This is content marketing. And it's an approach that's particularly well suited to the financial sector, where people are thirsty for quality content, as it often helps them to make an investment decision.

So, to succeed with digital marketing you must have a content marketing strategy in place.

But for it to be successful you have to produce content that people actually want to engage with. All those faceless investors I talked about are effectively providing their own financial advice by looking for useful and relevant stuff online. And, obviously, you want it to be your content they are looking at and engaging with. Because, if they've seen or read useful content from you then it's more likely they will look at the next thing you send out - all the way to the sale.

Yet the value of engaging content doesn't end there. Its importance is two-fold. Not only will good content draw people towards your firm and help convince them to invest with you, but it also serves as the bedrock of your digital analytics. As, by looking at your content and engaging with it, people give you data that can be analysed.

But what sort of content do investors want to see?

This is the billion-dollar question.

A penny for your thoughts

I can safely say, based on a career spent analysing these things for both ProFundCom and our clients, that the best performing type of content is thought leadership.

By that I mean a considered opinion, preferably from a senior figure in your firm, that offers some kind of help or guidance to the reader. This taps into a key aspect of content marketing – that it should offer help, rather than merely trying to sell. The concept of selling through useful content has been around for decades, and way before the digital age, which is why you used to find cookware firms sending out free recipe cards, and DIY chains producing guides to tricky home maintenance jobs. The theory being that by helping people, they are more inclined to buy from you.

And the theory of marketing through help and advice is equally applicable to the investment sector. If you provide helpful advice to people, they are more inclined to invest with you. Once again, this boils down to trust, as when you are seen to be offering help and advice – while expecting nothing immediate in return – then investors are more likely to trust you.

A good thought leadership piece can follow many different paths. For example, you could offer straightforward advice on the best sectors to be investing in for the coming year, or those to avoid. Or, you could take a stand against a common assumption and show how a different way of doing things would bring better results. You could also provide new perspectives on a current issue that is dominating the financial news or provide an insight into how things are likely to pan out in the future for investors.

Equally, don't be afraid to copy what your competitors are doing, as fast followers often do better than leaders. You certainly shouldn't avoid a topic simply because it has been covered by others, as that risks losing out on the pressing issues of the moment. I'm not saying you should plagiarise anything - you have to give your own views and ideally find a new approach or nuance that adds something fresh to the conversation. But by tackling a hot topic you can bask in the light of its popularity.

Thought leadership is unusual in that it actually provides a useful opinion on a subject, so is far more likely to be seen than other marketing material that just concentrates on sales or promotion. In fact, you should only make reference to your own firm or fund if it's directly relevant to what you are talking about, otherwise it undermines your attempt to show yourself as an impartial authority on a subject and thus defeats the object of what you are doing.

It's also more likely to be shared – certainly far more so than self-promotional stuff – and this is a crucial point. Few people would send a simple sales email to a friend, even if they did find it useful. But an interesting piece of investment advice, or an unusual perspective on a current theme, is something that interests people and which they may want others to see. Creating sharable content makes it even more valuable to you, as those on your mailing list, or visiting your website, or following your social media feeds, will start doing your job for you by spreading your content to others.

It's not necessarily easy to keep coming up with good ideas for thought leadership content, so you should have brainstorming sessions at least once a month with members of both your sales and marketing teams. This will help you develop and send out a steady stream of interesting and engaging content. This approach also ensures that you don't leave topic generation to the last minute and find yourself having to rush something through that may not be right for your audience.

What about performance?

When I talk about the value of thought leadership, I'm often met with a counter-argument that performance is more important.

The received wisdom is that performance is the main issue that guides investment decisions, Surely, you want to put your money somewhere that you know, because that firm is telling you, things are going well.

But this is simply not true. Time and again I've seen that content that focuses purely on performance fares relatively poorly.

That's because there's a problem with performance – it's variable. Sometimes you're up and sometimes you're down. You know that and potential investors know that. So, people simply don't believe an endless narrative about how well you are performing, as it is missing the bad news. And they think that you are obviously going to crow about it when you're doing well, but not so much when the needle's going the other way.

That's why, in my experience and what I've seen from countless clients, thought leadership content invariably outperforms performance-based content.

That's not to say performance shouldn't be part of your marketing strategy – it should – but it can't be all you talk about. And, although it may seem counter intuitive, you should also try to be honest about losses as well as gains. When you do that, people know they are getting the full picture, which helps to build trust (that word again) and respect.

You don't need to stop with thought leadership and performance when it comes to marketing messages. You can also mix in product information, news of events, company appointments, charity initiatives etc into your communication broth.

So, marketing can't all be about thought leadership but - believe me – it's that which will make the biggest difference in terms of raising and retaining AuM.

It's not what you say, it's how you say it...

So, you know what you need to be saying – but how exactly should you present it?

Let's start this topic by looking at how long a piece should be.

There is often a reluctance amongst marketers to go in-depth with content, as they get spooked by the oft-repeated claim that people have lost the power of concentration.

You'll often see the assertion, usually trotted out on a slow news day, that in the Twitter age of easily consumable bites of information, most people now have a concentration span so short it would make a goldfish blush.

So, to avoid people switching off, marketing content has to be short and sweet, right?

Wrong, as the whole shrinking attention span thing is complete poppycock.

Don't believe me? Then think about the last movie you watched. The average film is around two hours long, but people happily watch them. Hollywood isn't rolling out the ten-minute blockbuster to combat our apparent inability to take anything in.

Equally, the streaming revolution has ushered in the age of the TV binge, where whole series are consumed in one hit.

Or, if you want to move away from the screen, look at the enduring popularity of the book – in all its formats.

But what *has* changed in the digital age is the sheer number of distractions that assail us. From the time we wake up and go about our daily routine, our lives are saturated with various forms of digital communication. Texts, emails, alerts, calls and more come our way at every hour of the day. On top of that, there's work to be done, kids to be looked after, food to be cooked, fun to be had etc etc.

And languishing somewhere near the bottom of that list of priorities is the inclination to read your marketing content.

This again feeds into the inclination to keep things short, as the worry is that people are unlikely to read a long marketing email.

True. But they are equally unlikely to read a short marketing email, simply because they have better things to do.

The fact is that if they're interested, they'll read - no matter how long or short the piece. So, if you can say everything you need to say in 300 words then great, but if you need 3000 then so be it.

But no matter how long or short, you must make sure that you:

Grab them from the word go

It is important to tailor your content and messaging in a way that will instantly resonate with your audience and not come off as being too salesy or insincere – and you must do this from the word go. You have to quickly grab and hold their attention – do that and you can afford to talk at length about a subject. Fail to do that and you've lost them at the first hurdle, no matter how long or short the piece may be.

If you're sending an email, for example, then you first need to think of an interesting subject line that will serve as a hook and which is enticing enough to warrant an open. Avoid the mistake of writing an attention-grabbing headline that has little or no relevance to the subject matter of the email, as that will simply irritate the recipient. Instead, make your subject line a little taster of what is in the body of the email. This same advice holds for blog titles, press release headlines, etc.

Then, have an intro that tells people what they can expect from the piece, so they can make their mind up if they are interested or not.

Your content must also be an easy and engaging read. If it doesn't make sense, or it fails to hold the attention, then the recipient will quickly look for something more interesting to do.

So, keep sentences and paragraphs short. And never use a long word where a shorter one will do. For example, use 'buy' instead of 'purchase', 'try' instead of 'attempt', and 'time' instead of 'duration'.

Also, you must avoid too much jargon. But there is a caveat to that as a little bit of jargon often serves to underline your credentials and knowledge. So, there's no harm in using some investment jargon that you are sure the majority of your audience will understand – just don't take it too far. Similarly, with acronyms, if people understand what you're referring to then use them. You don't have to write Financial Conduct Authority rather than FCA, for example.

It's not we, it's you

Most content connected to business, and this is especially true of finance, uses far too much of words like 'we', 'our' and 'I'. 'What we do', 'our vision', 'I believe' etc etc.

Nothing wrong with a bit of that, but a lot of this sort of language means you are just talking about your business, rather than speaking directly to the people consuming the content - your potential clients.

An effective way to remedy this is to go through your marketing literature and change things around, so that sentences full of words like 'we' and 'our' are rewritten to talk about 'you' and 'yours'. This has the happy side-effect of making you write from the point of view of the reader, your potential investor, which will make you address their problems and concerns. And when people come across content that deals with their problems, they are more likely to engage with it and trust the source.

How it looks and how it reads

Structure and format are also important. If you're sending an email, for example, then one long block of text is extremely off-putting – nobody wants to read that, no matter how good the content.

So, split it up – have multiple paragraphs that are nicely laid out. You should vary the length, but always keep them relatively short, containing only one or two thoughts. This is *especially* important for the first paragraph.

Also, keep sentences as short as possible. Tests show the easiest sentence to read and understand is eight words long. A sensible average is 16 words. Any sentence of more than 32 words is hard to take in, as people forget what's been said at the beginning by the time they get to the end.

In short - if you want your writing to be read, make it easy for people to read.

Want to put images in your email? Fine, but make sure they are *relevant* – such as a picture of the writer in a thought leadership piece, or a chart or graph to illustrate investment trends. Avoid the trend of adding vacuous images, such as signposts and skyscrapers, that so often inhabit financial content, presumably as they are supposed to signify aspiration. It doesn't work, they're just annoying.

Check it – then check it again

Last point here, make sure you check and edit your content before it goes anywhere.

It's easy to make mistakes. But they can hurt your brand and make you look inefficient and disorganised, so it's important to weed them out of your content before it goes live.

Here are a few things you should do:

Change text appearance: When you proofread a piece of copy change the font, colour and size – you will concentrate more on the words when reading and mistakes will suddenly leap out.

Print it out: Reading from paper will enable your eyes to spot mistakes away from the harsh glare of the screen.

Read it aloud: This takes time but reading aloud forces you to slow down and look at each and every word, rather than just scanning the piece.

Once you have done all those things, just leave it. Put the piece to one side for a few hours, or even better a few days, then come back to it and have another look. You are then reading it with fresh eyes and can spot mistakes that previously may have eluded you.

Chapter 4 – Saving Souls And Choosing Channels

A guide to content distribution

David Ogilvy is a legend in the field of advertising and marketing. Known as the Father of Advertising, he wrote books that still sell millions and for decades ran a multi-national agency that worked with major brands from Schweppes to Rolls Royce.

He knew a thing or two, basically.

And it was Ogilvy who said this:

"You can't save souls in an empty church."

He meant that if people aren't listening you can't convince them of anything. That may seem obvious, but far too often, time, money and effort are poured into creating content that reaches few amongst its intended audience - as little thought is put into how to distribute it successfully.

Fact is, your carefully created content is worth *nothing* without an audience. So, you have to get it out there. But what are the best channels to use?

From our work at ProFundCom, both from the perspective of our own marketing and that of our clients, I see there as being three main channels that you need to use for content distribution – email, social media and web.

I'm going to use this chapter to go through each one. But first, an important point that governs all your content distribution - remember that repetition is not a dirty word. Not everyone is going to see each piece of content when you first post it. So don't be afraid to repost after a while and try it on different channels. Keep track of this by setting up a spreadsheet to show you what was posted when and where. Also, you can rework old posts when something changes, or a dormant topic becomes current again.

OK, down to the nitty gritty. And let's start with the daddy of them all:

Email

There are regular reports of the impending demise of email. This point of view suggests that it's an outdated relic of the early days of the web and usually rears its head when some new messaging innovation has launched, or when a study reveals that young people don't use email anymore, so it will soon die out (a theory that ignores the staggeringly obvious point that people's habits change as they age).

Don't believe a word of it.

Email is your star performer for any type of content distribution. It is the most widely used and preferred communication channel in the world and it just keeps growing. People depend on it – and that isn't going to change any time soon.

You don't have to take my word for this. During the first lockdown of 2020, when the real-world ground to a halt and everything went digital, we did a little bit of research here at ProFundCom Towers.

With the help of our friends at Greenwich Associates, we canvassed opinion to discover communication preferences for fund and asset management information. Our survey found that 92% of people wanted to receive data via email, above any other method.

The results surprised us all, as the general feeling was that the popularity of email would have taken a hit during the pandemic, particularly with everyone jumping on Zoom calls and pinging out IMs left, right and centre.

Not so. In fact, quite the opposite had occurred. Respondents pointed towards the sheer deluge of comms as a reason to turn back to email, as it was something they knew and trusted. You can get more detailed content through email, you can look at it when you want, and it's easy to file the information on your own system.

And here's another reason for you to use email, which is pertinent to everything I'm talking about in this book – it gives you a wealth of data to analyse. When you have a prospect in your CRM, you can find out exactly what you need to know about their wants needs and preferences by analysing how they interact with your emails.

But, of course, other communication methods are available:

Website

If someone is serious about investing with you, they will want to know as much about your firm and fund as possible. And that means that, at some point, they will visit your website.

But what will they find there?

If it's just a mass of bland 'brochure-ware' about where you're based, when you were founded, and the leisure interests of your senior team – then you're in trouble (does anyone really care that your HR Director is a keen marathon runner?). This does little to boost your worth in the eyes of a prospective investor who is looking for tangible reasons to back up their interest.

Instead, your website should give people things that are useful to them but are not obviously linked to your company and fund. And that means quality content.

Your site is a fantastic platform for your content. And that content doesn't have to be unique, it can be what you've already used on other channels. Once you've shared some good marketing content through email, you should then get it on your website, as this underlines your knowledge and expertise.

You can do this through a web library, for example – an ongoing collection of blogs, articles, videos etc that are all potentially useful and interesting to your target investors. You could even set up a proxy website, as many financial firms do, which is set up under another name to provide interesting thought leadership content and then funnels interested parties into your main site.

But, whatever you do, just make sure that all that valuable content you create and distribute eventually finds a permanent home on a website.

Think about it. If a prospective investor is browsing the web, then alighting on your site, which has a stock of well written thought leadership articles, this sets you apart from other firms that merely have promotional content as their web presence. What's more, this turns your site into a resource that people will visit to find reliable information on investing, rather than just to find out more about your company. This will also help you grow traffic to your site, which in turn means more potential investors are visiting it.

What's more, existing clients seeing this type of content on your site underlines a feeling of safety and security – as they can see they have their money with a company that knows what it's talking about.

So, you should put time, money and effort into creating an online resource that shows off the best of your content.

But you must also think about how to make your website user-friendly. This is vital, as a visitor is more likely to watch and read what's on your website if it's easy and simple to navigate and use.

Design is part of this – the fonts, colours and typefaces you use should make it easy to read the copy. And be careful not to choose style over substance, as any design element that makes it hard to read your content is going to be bad for business. For example, designers often want to present text in large, neat blocks, without spaces – but this makes it difficult to read, so should be avoided. The same is true of reversed out text, where light coloured wording is placed on a darker background. Instead, text should always be darker than the background, e.g. black on white.

You must also think about navigation – make it easy and intuitive to move around your site, so that visitors can quickly find what they are looking for. (I realise that sounds almost patronisingly obvious, but so many financial sites fail in this regard and have sites that are like some kind of fiendish digital labyrinth.)

Social media

There is a reluctance amongst many in our sector to embrace social media, perhaps because it seems so far removed from the traditional approach to financial marketing.

Well, tradition be damned - if you're not using social media then you're missing a trick. It's never going to be a mainstay of your marketing efforts, but it can play an important part in engaging and building trust with a client base that's looking to connect with you on a digital basis.

Social media sites are a great place to offer thought leadership snippets that link to longer pieces – on your website or elsewhere. You can also post links to your blogs, videos and podcasts, advertise upcoming webinars and events, etc etc.

Which platform is best? For the most part it will be LinkedIn, as users are fed a stream of fairly serious content there – so you tend to avoid the dancing cats, extremist rants and celebrity gossip that can fill other channels. You can also post articles that feature directly on the site, so it's a great place for thought leadership pieces that confirm you as a subject matter expert. Infographics, quotes, and informative content also perform well on this platform and are very shareable.

That's not to say Twitter, Facebook et al should be ignored. Although they don't have the same functionality and professional reach as LinkedIn, they can still be useful. Also, the social channels that you choose will vary based on your audience. So, do some research into where your existing and prospective investors are going online and make sure you establish a presence there, as you need to be on the platforms they are using. You shouldn't expect them to dig around and find information about your company – you should find them and make their life easier by sharing your knowledge.

But wherever you post, don't forget to use social media for the purpose it was intended - to socialise. It's vital to understand (although few firms seem to) that social media is a conversation. Yes, you're going to use it to promote your products and service – and your ultimate goal is obviously to raise and retain AuM – but that doesn't mean you can simply fire out content and forget about it, as people aren't going to come to you and start following you just on the strength of your name.

So, keep in mind that social media interaction is a two-way street – you must be sharing meaningful advice and opinions just as often as your audience, if not more. And you must interact with people - responding in real-time, acknowledging positive and negative comments, and sharing content, both your own and from other sources, that could help your followers. Keep an eye on your social media accounts to ensure you're responding promptly and properly to whatever is being asked or commented on. And always try and be personal and friendly – not cold and corporate – so you make the engagement as human as possible. Also, don't forget to use relevant hashtags, e.g. #funds, #investing #assetmanagement, to help people find your posts.

By actively engaging with your audience – and making sure you stick with it – you can cultivate an active community of prospective and existing investors who see you as a go to source of advice, so will come to you with questions and requests for support.

I can't leave the theme of social media without mentioning compliance. If you're in financial marketing, you know the rules about financial promotions and the necessity to include adequate risk warnings etc. But many seem to forget about compliance when it comes to social media. Indeed, if you ask a group of finance professionals what the FCA's rules are on using social media for marketing then you're likely to see lots of blank looks and shrugged shoulders. (I should know, I ask this question regularly.)

Not surprising, as the FCA's views on social media marketing are numerous and complicated. There is no room to go through it all here, but the one thing you should remember is that any social media post must be *stand-alone compliant*, so it has to have appropriate risk warnings within the body of the content. Brevity is no excuse, so there are no exemptions in regards describing risk or disclosing key information. And you cannot simply link to another website or post that contains all the necessary risk warnings – it must be in the body of the text.

Chapter 5 - Doing Alright, Getting Good Grades

How to harness the power of data analytics

After my opening chapters, I hope you can see the importance of digital marketing. The more quality marketing content you get out there, the more prospective investors you will attract and the more existing clients you will keep in the fold.

And by analysing the data you derive from your campaigns, you can significantly boost the worth of your marketing efforts.

But the theme of analysis deserves a bit more unpacking, as this lies at the heart of successful digital marketing.

Analysis is the key

Marketing data analysis, in short, is the science of examining how your prospective customers are looking at and engaging with your content. This has two valuable results:

Firstly, you can see the themes and channels that are performing best for you, which gives you the information you need to improve your strategy, so you can reach more people.

Secondly, on a more granular level, analysis allows you to see how each of your prospects is reacting to and engaging with your content. This helps you to single out those who represent a real sales opportunity, as they are engaging so much with what you're putting out. It also means you can single out existing investors who have stopped looking at your content, thus represent a redemption risk. This type of information is gold to your sales team. In fact, it's so important that I'm going to devote a whole chapter to it later on in the book.

But, for now, suffice to say that the information you derive from analysing engagement data is at the core of both your marketing and asset raising activities. If you *don't* have this type of information, then you are stumbling about in the dark.

Of course, gathering and keeping track of valuable engagement data, and acting upon it at the right time, is not without its challenges.

But, nice chap that I am, I've got something that can help you with that.

It's time to keep score

Many firms fail to use marketing analytics to its full potential due to a lack of organisation. I've seen this time and again – valuable data is flying about this way and that, but there is little thought to organising it and relating what you learn to your prospects and clients.

So, it makes sense to keep track of all this information and find out who is most engaged with your content. In the old days – and sometimes even now – this involved marketing teams looking at data and deciding which prospects were most deserving of the attention of sales.

But the process of triaging leads can be immensely time consuming when done manually. It also leaves a lot of scope for human error - and passing on the wrong leads to sales can waste your reps' time and strain the sales and marketing relationship.

This is where automation comes to your rescue, as you can set up lead scoring and grading systems within your CRM. The purpose of these is to automatically gather relevant data on all your prospects and clients and keep a score in regard to engagement. (Although, of course, you must ensure you are putting quality content out there – send out promotional rubbish that has nothing useful to say then your lead scoring efforts are dead in the water, as nobody is going to look at it).

At a very basic level your lead scoring could, for example, give one point for opening an email, two points for clicking a link, three points for downloading an attachment etc etc.

But it could be more nuanced than this. Opening certain emails or clicking on some links may hold more weight than others, so would merit a higher score.

It's a good idea to get your sales team involved when setting up a scoring system, as they are the experts on knowing when a prospect is ready for a conversation and will have a very valuable perspective on how to recognise and prioritise leads. So, both marketing and sales should come together to map out a system and work out what score should be assigned for each piece of content.

When you have a scoring system in place, you can link that to a grading process, where scores automatically place prospects into certain grades. This could, for example, range from a lowest E grade – for those who, although on your database, don't engage with any content, to an A grade for sales-qualified prospects who need to be contacted immediately, before the opportunity is lost.

Your system can then automatically push prospects and investors into grades as soon as they score a set number of points. A certain level of grade could mean that person is automatically pushed over to sales as a real investment prospect. Equally, consistent downgrading – through negative scores that reflect periods of inactivity – could push an investor onto the sales radar as someone who needs a call to prevent a possible redemption.

Scoring and grading can also work in warming up 'lukewarm' leads – those who open the odd email, maybe click on a few links and open an attachment or two, but never show enough interest to be useful to sales. But, you shouldn't just abandon these people – instead, have a scoring bracket that enters these prospects into a lead nurturing system, which automatically sends out content to them that's designed to pique their interest again. And if they appear to be interested in a particular product, the material should be relevant to that. Then, should these leads warm up further down the line, they will be pushed back into the sales process.

When used together properly, lead scoring and grading will streamline your sales cycle and ensure that leads are well qualified *before* they get to your sales team – saving money and time and, ultimately, boosting AuM. (You don't just have to take my word for this. A recent study by Forrester Research, found companies that automate lead management see a 10% or greater increase in revenue in 6-9 months.)

Account-based marketing

Before we leave this subject, it's also worth mentioning account-based marketing (ABM), as it links into what you are trying to achieve with scoring and grading.

The concept of ABM has been around for a while and refers to the practice of identifying major clients or prospects and then implementing marketing strategies that appeal to the specific persona and needs of these people. The theory is that by targeting prospects with material that's specific and relevant to them, you make them feel more valued and engaged and thus more likely to invest with you.

This concept works better for existing investors than prospects, as it's probably not worth investing time and effort into someone you only *think* may invest with you. But you can use scoring and grading to identify those big existing customers who show all the signs of wanting to increase their investment with you. Or clients who may not have a great deal of money invested but could still *potentially* be very valuable to you – and thus worthy of the extra attention that comes with ABM. There will undoubtedly be other criteria you want to apply, such as how long they've been a prospect or investor, the products – if any - they are currently investing in, their attitude to risk, and their attitude to marketing (as they may only deal directly with your relationship managers and would be annoyed by the extra attention from your marketing department).

Combining lead scoring and grading with these other criteria will allow you to build a profile for each potential prospect or investor, which enables you to fully assess their suitability for ABM and - if they make the list - to guide the type of communication you send to them.

Chapter 6 – It's A Trust Thing

How to build trust through marketing – and why it's essential to your business

I've mentioned trust a few times now in this book. And it's such an important subject - and so vital to the success of your content and your wider marketing - that we should look at it more closely.

Let's start with a cautionary tale that you may be familiar with:

Back in 1960s a man called Gerald Ratner inherited his father's small jewellery business. Within a few years he had transformed it into a retail empire, through a chain of shops offering affordable jewellery and glassware. The business, and Gerald, were flying high – there was a

Ratner's on nearly every British high street and the man behind it all had yachts, houses, limos and was rubbing shoulders with the great and good at high-society events.

Then, one unfortunate quip brought it all crashing down. As a guest speaker at an Institute of Directors event, attended by over 6000 businesspeople and journalists, he recounted his response to those who asked him how he could sell a cut-glass sherry decanter so cheaply. It was, he laughed, "because it's total crap."

Warming to his self-destructive theme, Ratner went on to say that his firm sold earrings for less than the price of a prawn sandwich, but that they probably wouldn't last as long.

The press, predictably, had a field day and Ratner's remarks were spread across front pages the next morning.

Even more predictably, this spelt doom for the Ratner's chain. Because, in one fell swoop he lost the trust of his customer base. How could they trust in the quality of anything bought in his shops? They couldn't – sales plunged, shares in the business dropped by £500million and within a year Ratner had been sacked as CEO and the company had rebranded.

The fact is that trust is a fundamental element of success in business. Without it, you have no real connection with your customer. And this applies to the investment sector more than most.

Think about it. Before you give someone your money, you want to know that they will act in your best interests and have the ability to achieve high returns for you. And both those things boil down to trust. In short, you don't give your money to someone you don't trust.

And once trust is developed, it establishes loyalty between client and company, which ties people in and secures them as customers for the long-term. Also, a relationship based on trust encourages positive word of mouth, which will bring in more potential investors.

However, there is a problem. Polls consistently place financiers way down the list of trusted professions – languishing at the bottom along with ad execs and politicians. The public image is one of greedy, faceless profiteers.

That is not a good look. And it makes it even more important to build and maintain trust.

But how – in a digital world where you rarely see people face to face anymore – do you do this?

Partly it's through quality, authoritative thought leadership content. This shows you as an authority in the field – and people trust authority figures (or at least ones that know what they are talking about).

But there are three other factors that, in my experience, are crucial in building trust:

Give your firm a trustworthy face

As we've already established, there isn't much trust in financiers. Even people within the sector sometimes find it difficult to trust each other.

So, it is perhaps astonishing – and certainly misguided - that so many funds and asset managers have smug, self-satisfied looking people facing their marketing material. This feeds into the very stereotypes that breed mistrust in the sector, as if the face of your firm is someone who seems to be the very embodiment of the greedy, self-serving financier then you're in trouble.

At the other end of the scale, many financial companies are faceless, which tends to suit fund and investment managers, as they like to be anonymous. But this in itself breeds mistrust, as it feeds into the media frenzy of unseen fat cats making obscene amounts of money.

Faces are instrumental in establishing trust, as we are social creatures and people buy from people. So, pick honest, helpful faces – the sort that people will *trust* - to front your marketing. Potential and existing investors want to see someone who looks open and trustworthy, which will underline in their minds that they are making the right decision with their money.

Be honest

The American adman Charles H. Brower once said that "Honesty is not only the best policy, it is rare enough today to make you pleasantly conspicuous."

Brower practiced what he preached - he was an advocate of telling the truth in adverts and pointing out to the consumer any seeming shortfalls in a product. His reasoning being that admitting to certain flaws would boost trust in the eyes of the consumer and boost sales.

A wise man. Honesty is quite rare in the fund sector. Companies often hide behind excuses and figures to try and make things look better or cover up their mistakes. But people see through this façade and reputations (and profits) are damaged as a result. Trust is based on truth – so if you're perceived to be lying, or at least not upfront with the truth, then you won't be trusted.

So, be honest and genuine with your prospects and investors, for example by admitting mistakes, or highlighting a downturn in performance and explaining why it may have happened. By doing this you differentiate yourself from your competition and build a reputation for being trustworthy.

Invest in your CSR

Corporate social responsibility (CSR) has become a trend over the past decade. And that can only be a good thing, as the world will be in a better position if firms act upon their responsibilities to the public and the planet and not just their shareholders.

But until relatively recently, CSR was largely more talk than action – a few quid bunged to a homeless shelter or hospice to pad out the annual report. Then cajole the CEO into going to the odd charity photocall and you're done.

But that has changed recently and now investors – especially younger ones – increasingly want to see that firms have a purpose or cause that goes beyond simply making money. This is a feeling that has grown during the Covid-19 pandemic. The crisis has hit so many people so profoundly - and left nobody untouched – that it has brought home the necessity for us all to pull together. Now, more than ever, it seems old-fashioned and profoundly greedy to just be concentrating on profit.

So, in the fund sector, it's not enough just to be trusted with money anymore. You need a CSR programme that demonstrates a real and demonstrable commitment to environmental and social causes.

This is fundamental to the issue of trust, as it's easier to trust a company that exists for a reason beyond just profit. If your company's corporate behaviour and values are not up to scratch, then many potential clients will look for somewhere else to invest their money.

So, to help build trust in your own firm, you must promote your charitable initiatives and community work - as there's absolutely no harm in making sure CSR also works for you in terms of positive PR. Make sure you talk about the good you do and publicise what is going on. You can achieve this by telling all your clients and the prospects on your database about your latest CSR initiatives. You can also publicise it on your website, talk about it on social media and announce it to the world through press releases and PR campaigns. The more your potential investors know about your CSR campaigns, the more they'll be inclined to trust you.

I practice what I preach on this point. At ProFundCom we have the ProFundCom Foundation, which we set up back in 2005 to help charities and communities in the UK and across the world. This wasn't a cynical decision – the foundation came about through a desire to help and give back – but equally I know that it helps us build trust with our clients.

There is no downside to a CSR programme, as nobody will refuse to invest with you on the grounds that you are doing too much to help charities and communities. But if you *don't* talk about the good you do, with specific examples, then it will count against you - as people just see you as greedy and profit-driven, which chips away at trust.

Another reason to shout about your philanthropic work is that, if you don't, you create a vacuum that can be filled by critics with an axe to grind.

This in turn can filter through the media and portray you in a negative light.

A word of warning to finish this point – don't try and fake it. There are still a few firms that talk a good game when it comes to CSR, without putting any real investment or effort into it. Don't let that be you – you will get found out and that will be fatal for your trust levels.

Chapter 7 - The Robots Are Coming...

The rise of AI and why it's good news for your digital marketing efforts

Like it or not, Artificial Intelligence (AI) is here to stay.

It's everywhere.

When you sit down in front of Netflix of an evening, it's AI that's suggesting what you should watch. When you ask Google Maps to direct you somewhere, it's AI that plots your route. And when you use your credit card, AI is watching to make sure it's a normal transaction – and you're not being ripped off by a fraudster.

Not everybody is happy about this and many fear that the unrelenting rise of AI will spell disaster for humankind. Stephen Hawking, for example, once said that "The genie is out of the bottle. I fear that AI may replace humans altogether...".

Far be it from me to disagree with the late, great Prof. Hawking, but I think the perceived threat from AI has been overblown and that most of the warnings you hear are just unnecessary scaremongering, especially when it comes to its impact on the workforce. The threat to jobs is perhaps why some people in fund marketing still shy away from AI - because of a fear that it will somehow 'take over' and lead to mass redundancies, or even render the whole marketing department obsolete.

It's true that AI – by its very definition - is doing tasks that used to require human intelligence. But, just like any computer system, AI needs people to be effective. It can also create work, as by quickly and effectively managing vast amounts of data, it in turn creates huge amounts of information for people to work on.

Certainly in the field of fund marketing, AI is very much a positive force. Think of it as augmented, rather than artificial, intelligence as it is there to help you, and will actually improve the capability of your staff – not get rid of them.

It has massive analytical power, so can be put to work in dealing with the torrent of data that will be rushing through your systems when you have a proper content marketing strategy in place. And the major benefits of AI are that it does this automatically (as long as you've told it what to look for) and incredibly quickly.

The possibilities are huge. But what exactly are they? How, specifically, can AI boost you digital marketing efforts?

How AI can help

As I've said, the main benefit of AI is its analytical capability. Digital marketing campaigns produce a vast amount of data, which is impossible to get on top of manually. But AI can quickly scour through it all to reveal the information that is most useful and important to you, so you can quickly gauge how well your campaigns are working and can identify the prospects and clients who are most likely to be sources of new investment.

You can also use your AI engine to automatically spot client personas as soon as they enter your system. Then your marketing and sales teams will be aware of their presence and can interact with these prospects as appropriate.

All this is great news for your ability to raise AuM. The other advantage is that it frees up so much time within your marketing department. People no longer have to do the painstaking work of sifting through marketing data to reveal insights about prospective and existing investors. Now, AI can do all this for you. So, your marketing team are left with the more important job of using the information gleaned through data analysis to boost AuM.

Other uses of AI

There are two other ways that you can use artificial intelligence that, while outside the general remit of this book, are worth mentioning - as they underline just how important AI is to your business.

The first is the communicative power of AI – as it can be used to chat to your clients and prospects through a chatbot on your website. When a prospect is on your site, you are engaged in a battle to keep them there. The longer they stay, the further you envelop them in your firm. And every prospect has questions, so having a chatbot there to answer them can instil trust and allay fears. Obviously, the range of questions a chatbot will be able to answer is relatively limited, but it could still mean the difference between someone staying on your site and clicking on a competitor's.

The other use of AI you should consider is its ability to spot fraudulent activity. AI systems no longer use the rules-based method to detect fraud, where activity that breaks certain rules is a red flag. Instead, an AI system can learn from data - instead of encoded rulesets - and analyse the features of *all* accounts and transactions, instead of just a few, to identify anomalous and possibly fraudulent behaviour. This is much more effective.

Enter the lone ranger

For the purposes of brevity – and in an effort not to bore the socks off you – I've so far used this chapter to give you a broad rundown on the benefits of employing artificial intelligence within your marketing strategy.

But I hope this approach doesn't suggest that setting up and running AI systems is an easy thing to do.

Because, believe me, it's not.

Certainly the concept and reasoning behind using AI in fund marketing is simple. It has vast analytical power that can make your job a great deal easier.

But introducing AI successfully into your marketing systems is anything but simple. Setting up, implementing and running artificial intelligence within your company is no easy task. It involves complicated technology that demands the attention of an expert.

And that expert is the lone ranger of the digital marketing world – the data scientist. Without a data scientist, you can kiss goodbye to any hope of AI making a meaningful difference within your firm.

But what is data science, exactly?

Perhaps the easiest way to answer this is to tell you what it *isn't*.

It's not data engineering, which is all about the back end of a system and actually building a database. It is not data visualisation, which is about presenting digital information in a way that makes it easily understandable. And strictly speaking it is not even data analysis, as that is the art of looking at past and present data to answer questions.

Instead, data science is all about what happens in the *future*. So a data scientist uses information to predict what is likely to happen further down the line and reveal what is most valuable and relevant to your future marketing and sales efforts. To do this they will harness and implement AI and set it to work on your data mountain, through measuring, optimising, communicating, experimenting and more.

Here are a few examples of data science in action:

1. Removing data noise

The simplest way to analyse engagement data is to look for the mean average - the piece of your content that's getting the most attention. But this can create a problem, as it can be skewed by having too much or not enough data, or by outliers – e.g. a webpage that is getting huge amounts of traffic but without any positive result. This is data 'noise'.

But a data scientist will more likely look for either the median average (the middle value of your data) or the mode average (the most common value). This cuts through the problems caused by mean averages. It removes the noise as mode and median are the most reliable indicators of what is having the most valuable effect, thus allowing you to concentrate your efforts accordingly in the future.

2. Standard deviation

If you hated maths in school, the mention of standard deviation probably sends a chill down your spine, but bear with me – I'll keep it short. Put simply, standard deviation is the opposite of data noise. In marketing terms, it tells you when someone deviates from the norm and looks at something unusual. For example, an investor who always looks at information on the same topic suddenly looks at something completely different. Immediately you have a cross-selling opportunity on your hands. Data science can identify these deviations for you.

3. Behavioural analytics

In simple terms this means understanding the client journey and how prospects and investors react to your content, which is obviously incredibly important and is mentioned often in this book. The beauty of data science is that it helps you with this process by tracking and analysing it all for you, to reveal behavioural nuances that help you divide your database into segments according to likes and dislikes. This helps you in your quest to send ever more tightly focused communications that are relevant to each individual, thus are more likely to be read and acted upon.

4. Clustering

In marketing terms, this means the concept of the word cloud. You can use data science to look at all the themes running through your campaigns and pull out certain words and phrases that are resonating most with your audience. This can be used to produce a word cloud that instantly shows what is working best – both the big attention grabbers and also the outliers that are creeping into the picture and may be worth some attention. This is a simple yet powerful way to see what the profitable themes are and where you should be concentrating your firepower.

5. Negative correlation

Another horribly mathematical phrase, which refers to a relationship between two variables in which one variable increases as the other decreases. But at least where fund marketing is concerned, this concept can be boiled down to one very useful function – data science not only uses negative correlation to calculate the prospects within your database who are most actively engaging with your content, but also those who have had little or no contact with sales.

This enables you to pull out the hot prospects and present them to your sales team, who then have an excellent chance of converting potential into actual AuM.

Look after your data scientists

As you may imagine, data scientists are hot property in the business world – they are needed in pretty much every sector and can command vast wages.

So, when you get one – you must look after them.

Partly this means you must be prepared to pay them the market rate – if not a little bit more.

But it's also about bringing them into the fold and making them feel part of the team. Forget about the myth of the data nerd, who just gets to work like an automaton and rarely speaks. Any data scientist worth his or her salt will be an engaged, inquisitive professional who is eager to learn about your operation and to interact with your team. And it's essential for everyone to realise and remember that data science is now a vital discipline of marketing. It's not something separate and removed – if you employ a data scientist then they need to be an integrated member of the team, included in strategy meetings etc, as the more they know and understand about your marketing processes, the better.

But there could well be a degree of resentment felt towards a data scientist by the rest of your marketing team, who may feel that their jobs are at risk. So, it's important to educate your staff and make it clear that data scientists are there to complement and build on the skills and experience of your existing fund marketing team.

Don't delay – get a data scientist today

If you don't already have a data scientist on your team then you must get one quickly. The possibilities of AI are increasing every day, but so is the complexity of handling this incredible technology.

So, recruit a data scientist and then do all you can to help them.

And if you want an example of how a data scientist can make a huge difference, you can go back to the infant years of the business world's favourite social media network – LinkedIn.

In 2006, the platform was struggling. People would join, but then fail to link with others on the network - which was kind of defeating the object. It was the idea of a data scientist to test the theory of a 'people you may know' feature, which encouraged you to connect with others who shared a former employer, school, university etc. It worked like a dream and this small change was instrumental in the huge subsequent success of LinkedIn.

Now, obviously you're not a running a social media site, but the principle here is that data scientists tend to be curious sorts who want to test stuff as a way of improving results. You must also give your data scientist room to experiment, as exploring speculative ideas is all part of the role. Not everything will work, but you should give them the space to try new things and tweak existing processes, as it can pay off big time.

AI is not a choice

My last point in this chapter is that the rise of AI in the fund sector – or in any sector for that matter - is an inevitability. So, you need to embrace it and run with it, otherwise you risk being left behind.

Remember that the rise of artificial intelligence is a positive step forward for your firm. The potential offered by AI is vast and by tapping into it and exploiting it you will become better able to market to both prospective and existing clients, which – of course – leads to more assets under management.

Chapter 8 - When Two Tribes Go To War

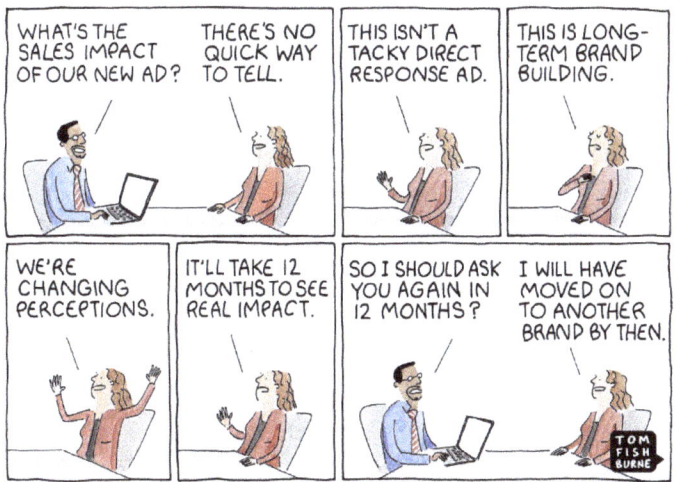

Why you must resolve the battle between sales and marketing

In Jonathan Swift's 18th century classic Gulliver's Travels, Gulliver becomes involved in a long-standing war between Lilliput and the nearby island nation of Blefuscu.

The dispute is bitter and has been going on for some time, but nobody can really remember how it started (it's eventually revealed to be a dispute over the best way to crack open an egg - Lilliput believes it should be broken from the small end, while Blefuscu contends it should from the big end).

This was Swift's way of satirising the conflicts of the age, which he saw as being small-minded, absurd, and ultimately unnecessary.

But I'm often reminded of the tussle between Lilliput and Blefuscu when I look at the interaction between sales and marketing departments. So often they seem to be locked in perpetual dispute, although nobody really seems to know why.

Marketing and sales have the same aim – to attract prospects and convert them to investors, ultimately generating revenue. Despite this, they often work as separate silos within an organisation. Marketing collects the leads, then tosses them over to sales and forgets about them. Sales works on the leads, but without asking marketing for supporting information or taking the trouble to provide constructive feedback on what has worked and what hasn't, and why.

This creates a serious problem, as although both teams are working to achieve the same thing – raising assets – how they can best get to that goal has different interpretations. Disputes arise over things like who gets credit for a sale, the quality of leads, how leads are distributed etc etc. Also, working independently means there is no tracking reviews going on, no consensus on key objectives, or strategic planning that involves both sides.

The crying shame is that any firm would do better were these two teams to work closely together. So, as part of your digital marketing strategy, you *must* bridge this gap and align your sales and marketing departments.

But, how do you do that exactly?

Be clear on definitions

Part of the problem is down to definitions, as – although the language used by sales and marketing departments is normally the same – the definition of certain terms is often very different. For instance, what the marketing team deems to be a sales-qualified lead and thus passes on to sales, may annoy the relationship manager who feels the prospect is not ready for a call.

The obvious answer to this is for both teams to make a mutual decision on what constitutes a marketing-qualified lead, a sales-qualified lead, a prospect, a cross-selling opportunity etc etc. This may take a while - and involve a bit of give and take – but when you've done it, you will have mutually acceptable definitions that are understood across the board.

And - if we go back a step - you need to have a big conversation about what even constitutes a prospect. Who are you going after? But the answer to this is usually different, according to whether you ask someone in sales or marketing. This can lead to a ludicrous situation where marketing is cultivating potential clients according to a set of criteria that doesn't bring in the prospects that sales ideally wants to be dealing with – those they know they have the best chance of converting into actual investors.

Alignment between sales and marketing on this point will ensure that you know who your ideal prospects are, where to look for them, and the type of language and content that appeals to them. This creates a more controlled path through the whole nurturing and sales process.

Having definitions agreed on by all is vital for the success of your digital marketing. You will be launching automations and instructing AI to look for trends and engagement stats that are based on these defined terms and the behaviour and data that lies behind them. If you don't get it right then it's going to lead to a lot of wasted time, money and effort.

Combine your metrics and reporting

Sales and marketing teams often have different ideas of what constitutes success. For sales, it's pretty simple – to an extent, the only yardstick of success they need is the solid numbers of sales made. There are nuances within that, of course, but that's what it boils down to.

But in marketing the waters are muddier, as there is not one overriding metric that dominates. Success is likely to be measured by stats like engagement rates, campaign performance and lead acquisition.

So, both teams have different ways of measuring and recording achievement. But this creates a problem, as a fantastic quarter for marketing may be a disaster for sales, and vice versa. Thus, it's important to agree on some shared metrics for success that tie in both sales and marketing teams - for example, the number of qualified leads that translate into sales. This encourages both teams to work together in pursuit of a common goal.

When it comes to reporting, you can bring both teams together through closed loop reporting - meaning that the data and information collected by marketing and sales is aligned and made available to both teams.

The information derived from closed loop reporting can be used to examine sales and marketing campaigns as a whole, rather than in a way that is only pertinent to one team. This ensures you look at a closed deal from a holistic viewpoint, showing the type of content that a successful lead interacted with and ultimately tying AuM to actual marketing campaigns. Then both teams can see every part of the jigsaw that has led to an investment.

This enables marketing to build on success, and lets sales see how leads behave throughout the funnel, which helps solidify the collaboration between the teams.

Start talking – and keep at it

Everything I have talked about in this chapter revolves around one central theme – communication. Without an ongoing discourse between sales and marketing you are not going to get very far. It's crazy that two such close departments do not communicate properly, but that is so often the way.

Don't let that happen – or if it's already happening, bang some heads together and make it stop.

You need to introduce regular meetings where everybody from sales and marketing come together to talk about issues, make plans and share best practice. And thanks to the ubiquity of collaborative tools like Slack, Trello etc, it is easier than ever to achieve. So, make sure you have both teams on a communal platform, where problems can be raised and resolved as they arise and everyone can add comments and suggestions. This process should be replicated all the way up the chain of command, so senior figures in both teams are in close contact and are monitoring the situation together.

Also, as remote communication is now so much a part of the sales landscape, it's simple for marketers to drop into sales calls and educate themselves on what clients want and need. This in turn enables them to develop more effective campaigns, which resonate with the target audience, as they know what is being discussed at the sharp end.

Put it in writing

You could introduce some sort of written agreement, that establishes a set of deliverables that each team has agreed to provide to each other.

This is a growing trend in business and it makes a lot of sense. A written agreement sets a level playing field for both teams and ensures that everyone understands what the goals are from the beginning. And when disputes do arise, which they inevitably will, the agreement can act as a rulebook to be referred to as a reminder of what the expectations are from each team, so they can stop bickering and start working together again.

An essential task

The bottom line here is that aligning sales and marketing is a must. To have two departments with such common aims working independently of each other is a recipe for disaster.

While it's true that technology is pushing sales and marketing ever closer together, this is often with much kicking and screaming.

Don't let it happen that way. Instead, manage the process proactively and put in the effort necessary to set up a collaborative culture that filters from the top down and draws everyone together.

Cohesive and collaborative practices can transform two struggling and bickering departments into a cross-functional team that acts as the powerhouse of your firm's asset-raising efforts. Because when sales and marketing align, the sales cycle shortens, and efficiency and productivity rise – as more leads are successfully closed and fewer opportunities are lost.

It may be difficult, it may take a long time, but do it properly and at some point you will get to the stage where it's second nature for marketing and sales to be working closely together.

Chapter 9 - The Secret Of Roger Federer's Forehand

How practice and learning can make your marketing better

It's difficult not to admire Roger Federer. Even if you don't like tennis, or don't like Roger Federer for that matter (let's face it, he is a bit smug), you can't but marvel at the way he plays the game.

Tennis can look so easy when he's on the court. There isn't the grunt and grind of the bulldozers of the game, like Nadal or Djokovic. Federer can make even a Wimbledon final look like he's having a knockabout over the washing line in his garden.

But I guarantee you that it all comes from hard work, dedication, practice – and learning.

Just like all professional tennis players, Federer analyses all his performances to see what he can do better – and what he should avoid.

And that's why he looks so effortless when he plays, as his mind is so quick to pick the best option. He knows what's going to work - and picks the right shot accordingly - because he also knows what doesn't.

Arguably his greatest strength is his forehand. Of course, he's got a great backhand too – and serve and lob and volley and everything else. But his forehand is where he really trashes the opposition.

And analysis will have proven to him that this is where he has been winning the most shots and where he should focus his game for the best results.

All the sporting greats – teams and individuals – in the modern era use performance analysis in this way.

What has this got to do with digital marketing?

OK, it's not sport. But the principle of improving performance through analysis is exactly the same.

This is one of the beauties of analytics – you can look at what you've done in the past and learn lessons that enable you to do better in the future.

The most obvious way to do this is through measuring engagement rates for your content, as this allows you to analyse what is working with your marketing - and what isn't. You can gauge the effectiveness of any campaign by tracking engagement levels, which allows you to constantly improve - as you learn what works and what doesn't.

Let's start at the simplest level – how many people have opened your emails. Even the most basic email management tool can tell you this.

If an email has bombed, then think about why that may be. It could be that a perfectly decent bit of content has been let down by a dull subject line – e.g. 'Fund Update', or the all too common but horribly uninspiring 'Monthly Newsletter' – that gives the recipient no reason to actually open an email. Try the same email with a different subject line and you could transform your open rates.

That's obviously a very simple example. But a more sophisticated system, such as ProFundCom (I'm not selling here, you could also use something like Tableau or Power BI), enables you to dive deeper into your analytics to reveal all sorts of trends and nuances

You can, for example, create models that make a big difference to your marketing efforts. For instance, by planning a graph that shows what works best at certain times of the year, or that shows you which content topics work best with existing investors, and which are more suited to prospective investors. You can also create a word cloud, as I mentioned in the previous chapter, which pulls out the words and phrases from your campaigns that are resonating most with your audience.

I could go on, but you get the idea – analytics can help you see what you need to concentrate more on and in what areas, and what you should probably ditch as it just isn't working.

Content and beyond...

The power of analytics stretches beyond content. It also lets you measure the effectiveness of channels, so you can see which distribution methods are working best for you. Knowing that helps you to distribute more effectively and maximise your audience.

One of these metrics is the geographical spread of your audience. Knowing where your prospects live gives you a handy insight into where you should be concentrating your marketing firepower. And while you may *think* you know where your prospects are based, only analytics can tell you for certain. It's not unusual to uncover hotspots for content consumption in surprising regions, which in turn can prompt a rethink about the best subjects to cover

This is something we track ourselves at ProFundCom and it often results in a change in focus. For example, our own recent geographical analysis revealed a growing amount of traction from people in south-east Asia – Hong Kong, Singapore and even Vietnam, whereas our key territories have always been North America and Western Europe. This suggested we had a ready market in those countries, so we created some campaigns specifically aimed at prospects in those areas – and we are building leads in south-east Asia as a result.

Another important, but often overlooked metric, is device usage. Are people mostly using mobile or desktop? iOS or Android? This is useful for optimisation and formatting purposes, as what looks good on a desktop – for example – isn't so great on a mobile phone.

Be like Mike

While performance analysis is essential, you must remember that it has no real value in isolation. Yes, it can tell you what you're doing right and wrong, but you must remember that you actually have to act on what you find and be prepared to adapt and change things if necessary.

If something's not working then it's no good just pumping out more of the same and expecting different results, no matter how good you get at it.

As another sporting great, Michael Jordan, put it:

"You can practice shooting 8 hours a day, but if your technique is wrong, then all you become is very good at shooting the wrong way."

Jordan was a famed analyst of team and individual performances and was always receptive to new ideas and ways of approaching the game whenever existing methods needed a rethink. This ability to adapt was one reason for his remarkable domination of basketball.

And, when you approach digital marketing correctly – and employ AI to dive deep into your data – you can do the same thing in respect to your campaigns.

Basically, you must use your analysis to establish *how* and *what* to improve. And this must be an ongoing task, as things can change so quickly in digital marketing. A new channel, for example, may take traffic away from what you're currently using. Or a thought leadership theme you are concentrating on may be losing credibility, so people are less inclined to look at content on that topic.

Things change incredibly quickly in the digital world, and for all sorts of reasons, but by keeping on top of your campaigns – and analysing the results – you can adapt and improve as you go along.

Chapter 10 - There's Gold In Them Thar' Digital Hills

How digital marketing analytics can boost your profits

As I've said, marketing is an intangible discipline.

But there are four pillars of data analytics that are as close to tangible as you are going to get, as they form the basis of successful sales conversations. This is, ultimately, what all your hard work is about.

I talked a lot in the previous chapter about practising and honing your content and strategies so that you reach more people. But it's still about the end result – bringing in AuM. And this is where all your efforts end up, revealing these four core pieces of valuable information:

➢ The prospects who are highly engaged with your content, to the extent that they look at pretty much everything you send their way. They open emails, download attachments, and click on links. But despite being so highly engaged, they have not yet had a conversation with your sales team. This is money waiting to be made, as these prospects are fruit hanging so low that you're in danger of tripping over it. Thus, these people demand the immediate attention of your sales team.

➢ The prospects who went away and *stopped* looking at your content but have now started up again. These are people who possibly went elsewhere, to a competitor, or maybe just had a rethink about the whole investment decision. Either way, they are back on your radar. They may or may not have had a previous conversation with sales, but this new activity suggests that they are once again looking at your firm – possibly after a bad experience with another fund – and are once again thinking of investing with you. They may well be cautious, but certainly merit a call from sales.

➢ Existing investors who are putting their digital hands up as a cross-selling opportunity. This would typically be because analysis reveals them to be looking at products they don't currently hold, which suggests they are happy with how you are handling their money and could be looking to branch out. So, a quiet word from sales could lead to an increased investment.

➢ Your current investors who have suddenly *stopped* looking at and engaging with your content. This is information that is all too often ignored, or just not even looked at. But it's actually vital, as when this happens it's a red flag, as it suggests they may be dissatisfied with your service or be concentrating on what the competition is offering. Either way, a well-timed call with your sales team could prevent a redemption.

These four categories of people represent the ultimate aim of your digital marketing efforts.

Everything you do is designed to reveal the intentions of the prospects and clients on your list. This both enables you to send more targeted messages and gives your sales reps the intelligence they need to have a conversation that results in the raising or retention of assets.

Basically, this is the gold.

How to show off your wares

But your glittering prize is worth nothing unless it's in the hands of sales – as they are the people that can turn it into something genuinely valuable in the shape of AuM.

So, you set up a lead deck within your CRM, which gives your reps the crucial information they need at a glance. The information on a lead deck should include where prospects are based, what is – and is not working, theme analysis to show what people are particularly interested in, trend analysis to show what they have looked at in the past, and even which digital touchpoint actually brought them into the fold in the first place.

Your deck should be optimised so that a rep can bring all this information up with just a few clicks – don't expect them to be digging around for it. Then, pertinent information is always to hand and they can strike while the iron is hot.

A quality lead deck means your sales reps can instantly bring up a list of prospects and see information taken from across the CRM that shows key data about each person - without having to jump between various spreadsheets and tools, with all the hassle that involves. This is a massive advantage before and during a sales call, as it enables a rep to show the investor they understand their problems and interests, which helps to instil trust.

Chapter 11 - Know Your Worth

How to measure and demonstrate marketing ROI

"Know your worth. People always act like they're doing more for you than you're doing for them."
Kanye West

I'm sure Mr West didn't have the fund marketing sector in mind when he said this, but his words should serve as a warning for anyone in our sector.

If you're in marketing and you don't know your worth then you can't defend yourself, or your marketing efforts, properly. And you risk being seen as a department that is being carried by the rest of the firm and that has a vague and undefined purpose.

Part of marketing's image problem is that it is an intangible discipline. Its purpose is to create and drive demand, but how do you actually show that when it's the sales team that takes all the glory?

I started this book by saying that when belts need to be tightened, the axe often falls on the marketing department.

That's a needlessly destructive act that will only do harm in the long run.

But it's borne from the fact that firms throughout the land – and in pretty much every sector - don't understand how much their marketing department is worth to them, which is stupid.

But, equally, marketing departments often don't understand what they're worth to the company, which is unforgivable – and often fatal. Because, when the axe is hovering, how are you going to argue your case?

You must understand the worth of marketing to your firm and be able to back that up with solid figures.

This is a simple concept, but so few in marketing seem to grasp it properly. They bumble way in their own little bubble, in happy ignorance of the hawks who are circling from above - and they only think about it when it's too late.

The metrics you need to show

When asked to justify your worth – and by extension your very professional existence – what sort of stats do you need to be showing?

Let's start with your bread and butter – prospect analytics. Your job in a marketing department is to bring new clients into the fold, so you need to be able to show how well you are doing this.

You can break this down into four main components:

- The number of new prospects you have on your list
- The number of active prospects on your list who are engaging with your content
- The number of highly engaged prospects on your list who are engaging *regularly* with content
- The number of prospects you have recently emailed

You also need to be able to relate this to the content you are showing these people and how well it is working. The key metrics in this regard are:

- Is the distribution group growing?

- Are the emails convincing and leading to positive action?
- Is the wider content working?
- What is the dropout rate from your mailing list?

Your friend the data scientist can help with all this, as they can create dashboards that give an analytical overview in an interactive and visually appealing format. This can be particularly helpful when giving senior management an overview of a campaign, or ongoing marketing activity.

However, a snapshot of all these metrics is pretty meaningless, so you must be able to demonstrate growth over a period of time for them to work in your favour. And don't worry if you have a small list, these stats are still relevant and collectible.

Show them the money

If you are lucky enough to be reporting to a C-suite who understand and value the role of the marketing department, then the stats outlined above may be all you need.

But, frankly, you probably aren't that lucky. In the end, money talks so chances are you must also link your activity to money through the door – to funds raised. Or indeed to money saved through funds retained.

You can obviously point to the four pillars of marketing data I mentioned in the last chapter, but that still doesn't fully justify your worth. It merely shows that you are revealing things that *could* be useful in terms of bringing in and retaining AuM.

Thus, anything you can show that directly links your efforts to actual fund-raising activity is going to be very valuable.

So, when you are in front of the big, bad CEO - who is just itching to find a reason to jettison marketing and save a wodge – you do yourself a massive service by showing them the complete journey of a sale. Show them the thought leadership content that brought that client into the fold. Show them the nurturing emails that kept them interested and were specific to their needs, which you were able to deduce by analysing engagement. Show them the lead deck screen that the sales rep referred to during that crucial conversation.

Show all this and you clearly display your worth - and you also make it clear what *couldn't* and *wouldn't* have happened without the marketing team.

And this also ties into what I was saying about aligning with the sales department, because the more closely you are aligned to sales, the easier it is to relate marketing activity to sales success. Also, by keeping marketing and sales close you make it difficult to make cuts, as sales can see they will be negatively affected by any damage to the marketing department.

Be prepared

Last word on this and it's a vital point:

You should be prepared, at any point, to be able to show your worth and have all the necessary stats and figures ready to show.

Because if you wait until asked to think about these questions, it may already be too late. You *must* be ready.

Even better, make a point of asking to be in front of the board. This can only work in your favour, as it puts you in control of things. And anything you can do to highlight your work and achievements to internal stakeholders will lead to recognition for the work that you have done.

Chapter 12 - Psychology 101

Why understanding how people think will benefit your marketing

You can't write a book on marketing without mentioning psychology, as any buying decision is driven by what goes on in the head.

And while we may like to think of ourselves as rational, logical beings who are completely in control of our choices – it's simply not true. Much of our behaviour is governed by psychological mechanisms that are working subconsciously and guide us without us registering it.

In fact, you could write a *whole* book on the subject. It is a huge and fascinating topic and one that I can only touch on here.

But even a rudimentary understanding of what makes people tick will allow you to communicate more effectively with existing and potential investors and drive asset growth.

So, I'm going to pick up on three aspects of marketing psychology that will help you to reach your prospects and clients better.

Use social proof

This is the principle that says that, when selecting a product or service, people are far more likely to choose one that others have positive experiences of using. This is a psychological trait that's rooted in evolution. Humans have prospered from the ability to copy what others are doing, so it's hardwired in us to follow the herd.

Not all businesses need to worry about social proof. For example, say you want to open a pizzeria. If you open up in Leicester Square in London, then your shop will be packed every day of the week, mostly with tourists who you'll never see again. So, you could afford to sell overpriced pizzas made with cheap and nasty ingredients and still turn a profit, as your customer base is changing all the time and you don't rely on people coming back for more. In fact, in terms of making money, it's better for you to rip off your customers. (And if you've ever had a slice of pizza in Leicester Square you'll know that many follow this mantra.)

But say you open your pizzeria in a remote country town. There, you'd better make sure you sell decent food at a fair price as you have a limited customer base where word spreads. So, sell good pizzas and customers tell others – and you thrive. Sell overpriced rubbish, then word will get around that your pizzeria should be avoided - and soon you won't have a business.

Your firm – especially if it's small or medium sized – is that country pizzeria. You have a relatively limited pool of prospective clients – and they are far more likely to invest with you if they've heard good things and will avoid you if they hear bad stuff. Basically, you need a reputation that is good enough to both keep assets under management and attract fresh money.

So, you must work hard to please your existing clients and then use marketing to spread the positive feedback you get to attract others.

Avoid looking cheap

A few years ago, a fancy new wine shop opened near to me. And one day an invitation to a tasting popped through my door – it was in a thick red envelope and was handwritten in gold pen.

Impressive. And I duly went to the tasting, which was thronged with people, many of whom bought expensive cases of wine. But a handwritten invite is a costly way of pulling in the crowds - would it not have been cheaper and easier to simply send an email?

Of course, but that would have singled out the shop as a company that does things on the cheap. And few people would have gone to the tasting. That's because people attach importance to things that appear to have taken effort. A handwritten letter takes effort – both in terms of time and cost. An email does not, so the perceived value is much less.

This is a psychological trait that we share with animals. Male creatures that put a lot of effort into courtship rituals are more likely to attract a mate, as that suggests they will be prepared to put in the hard work necessary to look after a female and a family.

Similarly, a firm making an effort with marketing material suggests to prospects they will be treated well as a customer.

And this is an important lesson to learn in respect to digital marketing. One of the beauties of this way of communicating is that it's cheap. But that also means you are in a fight to show people that what you are saying is of value.

This ties into what I was saying earlier in the book about the need for quality content. If you put thought, effort and money into your marketing, then you look as it you have made an effort - and will be rewarded by higher levels of engagement. Skimp on what you're doing and people are more likely to ignore what you're saying.

Lower the risk factor

As humans, we tend to favour decisions that seem to have little or no risk, as these choices protect us from harm. This is part of what has made us so successful as a species.

So, we make decisions based on how much harm we could potentially come to, even if that risk is very small. This is why, for example, the practice of hitchhiking has largely died out, as people are worried about picking up a murderer. Although the chances of a homicidal maniac getting into your car are extremely low, we've all seen too many horror films – and the *fear* of that happening is enough to stop people giving lifts to strangers.

Reducing risk is an incredibly important aspect of a buying decision – probably more so than the opportunity of gaining something. As somebody clever, I forget who, once said - 'Man fears to lose more than he hopes to win.' Marketers know this, which is why you see so many campaigns that promote money-back guarantees and risk-free trial offers. The more you can reassure customers and potential customers of zero – or at least limited – risks, the more likely they are to take the course of action that you want.

Now, given you are in the investment game, you're dealing with decisions that are inherently risky - and it is both a moral and legal requirement to make that clear. But you can use your marketing content to put your prospects' minds at rest about the *level* of that risk. Point out positive results and trends, but also highlight the experience and knowledge of your staff, the stability of your firm, or the promising prospects for a particular sector.

Basically, the safer people feel the more likely they are to invest with you.

Chapter 13 - Crystal Ball Time

Five predictions for the future

OK, we're nearly done.

But before I leave you, I'd like to make five predictions, all based on what's been discussed in this book, on how things will change over the coming years and what you can do to capitalise on them.

1. Firms That Prosper Will Be Firms That Work Together

I've talked at some length about the need to align sales and marketing. But actually this applies across the board and the need to work together is more important than ever.

The work-from-home revolution that started in 2020 - sparked through necessity by Covid-19 - taught us the need to work together as a team. This may sound a little clichéd, but suddenly having a whole firm working from home brought the importance of inter-departmental cooperation into much sharper focus. Suddenly, you couldn't rely on a colleague next to you to know what's going on in the sales department, for example – it was down to you. So, everybody discovered the need for contacts and cooperation across a firm. And instead of mutual distrust across the board, there has been greater cooperation between marketing, sales, operations, investing etc.

I hope it's obvious that sales and marketing must come together as they are working on a common cause – that of raising and retaining assets. But actually, *everyone* who works at a fund – whether they are talking to clients, analysing data, handling payroll, or making the lunchtime sandwiches – must understand that that is their ultimate reason for being there. Without it, there is no money, no firm and no jobs.

2. Investing in your IT is an investment for the future

During the pandemic I found that the firms that did particularly well had concentrated on four key aspects of their IT infrastructure – they leveraged the cloud, built flexibility, used collaborative software, and made it easy for all staff to gain access to relevant systems, wherever they were based.

The major benefit of all this was they developed a remote, digital way of working that was effective and efficient. Of course, all firms did it to a certain extent – there was no choice - but those that did it well are going to reap the rewards in the future.

It seems highly unlikely that we'll go back to the days of a whole firm descending on the office each day, particularly as it's such a costly exercise. And the theory that people are more productive in an office environment is not borne out by the evidence. A recent study involving 16,000 staff found that those allowed to work flexibly from home increased their productivity by 13%. The flexible workers also reported higher work satisfaction and took less sick leave than their office-bound counterparts.

That's not to say working in an office doesn't have benefits – it helps to build relationships, encourages collaborative working, combats loneliness and more. However, it also has multiple drawbacks – constant interruptions, irritating co-workers, wasted time travelling, and the cost and hassle of keeping a large office infrastructure running. On top of that, working from home has become ingrained - so capable, flexible IT systems that facilitate remote collaboration are more important than ever and will help firms grow.

3. Effective digital communication will enable marketing reach to increase

The temporary end of face-to-face meetings has made everyone happy to meet remotely.

If you are based in South-east Asia, for example, why did you care if you had a Zoom call with someone in Singapore or London? Geography suddenly became much less of a barrier. And those firms that adapted quickly and seamlessly to this, with good tech, became particularly popular as they were well equipped to reach out to prospects on a global scale.

And this ties into what I was saying about using analytics to monitor geographic spread. When you use analytics to reveal the hotspots of where your marketing is reaching, you can tailor your content accordingly and send out region-specific messages to these people, which will bring in new sources of revenue.

4. Smaller firms will use digital marketing to prosper

Smaller firms – those with £5bn or less under management – are currently facing a double whammy of challenges. The figures show that less money is coming into these companies, and more redemptions are flowing out, in comparison to larger firms. That's probably because people are less willing to take risks during a period of major uncertainty, thus go with big names they know.

This means that small firms are going to have to work harder for less reward. But strong digital communication and marketing can help you face this, as it's a way of setting yourself apart and building trust. This is absolutely essential during these troubled times, when people are looking for solidity and reassurance.

So, you must have a solid content marketing strategy that places thought leadership content at the forefront. Create this, then distribute it properly and intelligently through email and other digital channels and it will have a positive effect on your ability to raise and retain assets. This is the general message of this book and is applicable to all firms of all sizes. But I'm seeing that it is the small to medium sized firms who are best placed to take advantage of this, as they are more flexible, and have smaller and more focussed marketing teams. This makes them better able to adapt to what data is revealing and give clients and prospects more of what they want to see and less of what they don't.

I predict that the impact of this will be the tide turning and more money coming into smaller firms over the coming years.

5. The tech brands are coming

About twenty years ago something exciting happened in the book sector. You didn't have to go to a bookshop any more to buy your books, as you could buy them over your computer through this new website called Amazon.

Fast forward two decades and that company is a household name with a foothold in almost every aspect of consumer goods – from books to tech to groceries – as well as online streaming. There's not much you can't buy through Amazon. And the reason it can move so quickly and decisively into new markets is through the power of brand. Given Amazon can send you a new printer cartridge within a day, you don't doubt its ability to, for example, provide a match day experience from the comfort of your home when it comes to live football. You trust the brand to deliver.

As a result, Amazon is one of a handful of big tech brands – along with the likes of Google, Apple and Microsoft – that increasingly dominate our lives. And they are using the power of their brand to expand into new sectors. Healthcare is a good example. Google, Amazon and Apple are all pouring money into health, as they see it as a sector where money can be made.

And how long before the digital giants have the fund and asset management sector in their sights?

The same three firms - Apple, Amazon and Google - are all tipped to enter this market soon. They don't need to build an actual infrastructure, which is the beauty of their business model – they just need a fund in a marketplace. And they have vast customer bases to tap into that know and trust these brands.

So, it is more important than ever to build up your own brand and make sure it's as strong as possible and is synonymous with good advice and outstanding service. Do that and you protect yourself from the disruptive power of the big boys, as you will build a cohort of loyal investors who know and trust your brand, thus are less likely to look elsewhere.

The last word

I have, I hope, given you food for thought in this book and provided ideas and information that will help you improve your digital marketing efforts and make a real difference in regard to raising and retaining assets. We can all get better at marketing, and that applies to me as much as anyone else.

The bottom line is that when you take the time to communicate properly with your prospects and clients, in a way that is both helpful and insightful, then you will interest them and engage with them. And when you analyse the results of this interaction – and apply what you learn – then you massively increase your ability to raise and retain assets.

This is the potential of digital fund marketing. And adapting to this way of working is a necessity, rather than an option. Those that fail to do it quickly or thoroughly will soon get left behind by the competition.

By contrast, when you embrace this opportunity and invest time and effort into building a proper digital marketing strategy, you will reap considerable rewards.

About The Author

Paul Das is the Managing Director of ProFundCom, which he founded back in 2003 to provide digital engagement analytics that directly benefit sales and marketing processes in financial institutions. You can find more of his musings on LinkedIn.

About ProFundCom

ProFundCom is the leading digital marketing platform for finance. It brings all elements of digital activity – email, web and social media – into one place through a versatile and powerful software platform designed specifically to support sales and marketing for hedge funds and asset managers.

The company has offices in London, New York and Geneva and currently works with over 50 retail and institutional fund providers, boutiques and private banks across the world.

CPSIA information can be obtained
at www.ICGtesting.com
Printed in the USA
LVHW071737150323
741694LV00007B/215